Underserved, Unearned

She had a reckless mind, a heavy heart, and a beautiful soul.
Although she gave belief to the thought she fell from it,
she came to know new days, a new heart.
Her hope chest always full. She relishes the plumeria's bloom.
It is divine the way she carries her grace.

Water in My Wine

Emmanuella Raphaelle

JOURNAL JOURNEY

Dedication

Have you ever been touched by an angel?
The ones who live and breathe among us. In the world,
in our heart, in the streets, from the sky. Have you ever
been cut deep or hurt-full, broken open to healed whole?

These words belong to the ones who came to hurt
and heal us, love and liberate us. For their touch has
been so profound in our way. Their impressions leave
us marked and changed for a different life. This is
dedicated to people. We are all worth loving.

Acknowledgments

I acknowledge I would not be me without the gifts of you.
I acknowledge I would not be me without the lessons
from them. I acknowledge I would not be me without
the grace of Father God. I acknowledge everyone and
all who have inspired every verse and stanza in me.

Thank you for inciting me to poetry.

"Pour Water in Your Wine"

With each yesterday gone and tomorrow come, I learn to become more and more strong in my resolutions. The purpose is to be aware, alert in the breath of life, feeling what it brings and passing through. I believe I am supported in this experiment. Today's message. My God. I was kindly reminded. I am a survivor. I was preserved. I went in as water and came out as wine. Really incredible, considering the maternal being has, for years, impressed upon me to pour water in my wine. I will do no such. Why discolor or tamper with my flavor? Why settle down and become what others want me to be, when I am perfect in the eyes of the One who created me?

From *"After the Affair, Re-Membering"*

Five words she gave to me.

She would give them intermittently or constantly. At the height of or at a low point…mother-knows-best could use any occasion to drill those five words into my being. Little did I know, all the while I was resisting them, her spell would conquer within the universe persisting after me.

"Pour water in your wine," she said. "You are too…" (fill in the blank). Only her words were not English but of French decent. A creole dialect I thought insulted my intellect. Why would I pour water in my wine? I'm already fine. But mother knew best.

As life would have it, her words went before me. They were not empty; they turned every corner a few moments ahead of me. They drew every circumstance near to me. They conjured every lesson from a human designed specifically for me. Like a spell, she casted process over me. Like a spell, she casted maturation over me. Mother dearest knew I enjoyed a fine glass of wine. And like a fine skin of wine, I would be made to endure, to age and to pour.

As winemaking is a process, so am I. As the grapes of wine endure crushing and pressing and agitation, so have I. My dilemmas crushed and squeezed matter out of me that very well needed to be extracted from me to produce a finer me. The clarification came upon me years ago when I started writing *After the Affair*. It became crystal clear to me, I was not being instructed to dilute my quality. But life harvested me at a point when I was doing too much. It seems it was inevitable; my life events would ferment and mature me for such a time as this. All my resistance, shed tears and heart lessons promulgated into history for my destiny.

Water in My Wine is written in homage to my mother. There is a time to be mellow, there is a time to be port. There is a time to be bittersweet and there is a time to be fine. I finally got it, Mommy.

* * *

Beyond this page, you enter into the soul of every meditation, every rousing thought or verse of poetry that flowed through me when my character lived, died, and rebirthed among those years. Learning to heal, love, forget, forgive, restore and rejuvenate looks like this.

At times, reading the chronicles from my past
feels like walking on shards of broken glass
barefoot
but for forgiveness and grace
but for progress and a new again
and another again
and a different again
I am poetry in motion
I don't have to cringe at the mess I was then
I can love the woman becoming all the more now

Wisdom...

A young girl growing up,
Momma told me
find a man who loves you
more than you love he
And to this day,
young girl grown older
none can compensate
I love alone

But this is not the inheritance
I will give to the daughter
birthed from me

and for that matter
any other she...

Interlude

Once our marital bed
now just a mattress
stained of muted tears
unanswered prayers
and dried up cum from the years
of missionary work I gave
just to keep his mouth shut

For all the times we lay in the bed
beside our burdens
tongue-tied,
for no words could take the cold off our shoulders
for how you hollowed my insides
shooting blanks...
couldn't fill me with love
I'd like a new body with no remembrance of you

A new bed, a new room,
a new head space is overdue
And can I get a new heart
too?
For who knew
that with the one I said "I do"
would come my greatest love lesson
I would live the meaning of the adage
Love the one who afflicts you

Innocence

And there was an innocence in me
I can still see it vividly
when I look toward back then
that day I wore the off-white capris
that sunny day I said "I do"
in the corner of a courtroom

A hopeful innocence in marriage,
that day I held his hand
I expected so much from "I do"

I was childlike then, light of heart
I was giddy then, bashful and smiling

Promised in my youth
I looked up to a husband then,
I liked to stand beside him
I felt safe in his shadow
But he was just a man

And my innocence I gave
He was my first everything
How could I know he would become my first nothing
And when innocence began to slip through my fingers
I almost wished I could be a virgin again

A virgin to wonder
A virgin to trust
A virgin to closeness
A virgin to holy intimacy in our carnal matrimony
Who could crave till death do we part
Loyally

An artless form of feminality
I was to be defiled with deceit
And sullied with regret
Impregnated with loneliness
I would never be pure again

The veil, soiled and pilled,
it hangs from somewhere over there
with the white dress I never wore
Traded it for a cap and gown
from the university of adversity
I know different now

I may have surrendered unwillingly my innocence
but I steadfast, kept resilience
learned the fine art of temperance
came to own my righteousness
And live to give love with my presence

with all the
forever
we have in now
we should learn
to make love
in the *our*

the time is always now for every hour to know our love

Holy Matrimony

Words she gave to a Husband:

Realize the weight in your hand, Man.
Hold me close and tender.
I am rare. I am precious. I am real.
Hold me real...
I have so much to give you, share with you, be with you.
I have so much...
Taken from your rib, please understand and bear with me.
See into me, become me. Protect me, love me.
Man, you are so capable.

Realize, you would not be given me if you were not pre-
pared or equipped to go the way with me.

I am not machinery to be manhandled.
I am woman to be tendered, kissed, caressed and measured
with uncontainable love.

Meet me in my head.
Join me in my heart.
This is my sincere request to you.

Love Me with Your Clothes On

Look into my eyes
admire me,
what do you see
Let us touch faces, please
kiss my neck, my shoulders
embrace all that I am
Hold my world in your hands
Kiss my leg, my ankle
(now) come back up
Kiss me between my breasts
near to my heart
where it pumps,
hear its sound
I know you can love me naked
but today, tonight, before we fake it
let us make it
Let us love with our clothes on

Romance me with your vision, your dreams
let our destiny become a reality
Before we entertain the fantasy, the fallacy
Love me in your attire
dig me deep
but be sweet
Let us journey higher than the ooh and aah

of the orgasmic power
Meet my words with sincere lips
agree with me
Speak your love language into my reach
give me something, strong, to hold on to
Let us not collapse
Not obscene, clean
no ordinary love, not between the sheets
we know the songs
Let me see you naked with your clothes on

Disrobe your distress,
remove the fear, no shame
let me see your underwear
The wear under your heart bleeding
where emotional scars tear you apart
Let me love you with my clothes on

Let me touch you with no hurt on
let me feel you naked as you are
humbled and wounded
make me tremble from your secret thoughts
Make me love you with your robe on
let me take in all your glory
Invoke me, touch me, breathe me
just love me, real love me
vulnerable, honest, non-resentful, in light love me
Love me with your clothes on

We don't need a condom for this
we don't need to protect from this
no birth control or contraceptives
You need not penetrate into me
a false knowledge of who you be
our bodies need not meet to attain a false sense of "we"
We don't need to build architecture from this
let the armor fall down,
let the love reign down
We can give birth to our happiness

We just need to love,
the uncomfortable to comfortable for real love
the grow you to grow me: us love
Love me like this every day in the details love
With all your clothes on
our union is of holiness
God is in this!

He Knows Me Not

But, do you know me
the nights are lonely without you
and when you are around
your company arouses my misery
the change I want to see
you stifle it in me
to your heart I beg, to your mind I plead
I want you to want me
intellectually, introspectively
passionately, urgently, willingly
How do I not appeal to your sensitivity
Man, how do you not want to know me
in the wildest of ways,
or even on the mundane days
I thought you would cover me,
betroth your devotion to me
but too often I find myself questioning:
Do you love me?

Teetering on the Surface

How do I hate this house
this table
even this pen, this paper
it continues to write of our nothingness

How can I hate to feel
to sit in the grief of my humility
Is this humility?
How can tears filter through hope
And from where comes hope when my faith is decaying?

Yet he slumbers in peace
with no dis-ease
He perceives not my necessity
to connect with his authority, his virility, his potency
even a fury
any emotion to prove he breathes

Any word to create the shelter
any word to live and grow inside of
he offers none
Even a gesture to mean I'm for you, be for me
but he does not concede
his quiet confesses a truth to me…

Tired and sleepless
on the kitchen table I find me
compiling pieces of sage advice, scriptures and old quotes
scrambling for a different testimony

Perhaps I will find it in loving me
love keeps no record of wrong
so where is my love for me?

In every passing moment
with every word spoken
and the ones left unsaid
we are choosing
to coalesce
or disembody
each other

devote to words that choose togetherness

Re-Member Me

but Man,
if you remembered I carry your rib within my flesh
bearing my bones
perhaps you would show more respect for me
with loyal reverence
you would hold us…

Have you forgotten?
I am from you

Intermission

I love the lull of morning
to watch dawn quietly breaking
spilling the colors of life
into a new day unfolding
opalescent peace presses its way
through sleepy clouds
filtering down
iridescent joy
all around, the hum-drum of wonder waits
expectantly for an anxious heart
to open, to beckon, to foresee
It is a perfect day to live

Bliss from the quick glance of a sky
and a cloud through the foliage of a majestic tree

Interlude

He was a tempter,
a collector
of things not his
not a keep-her
or a love-her
only a use-her...

because I didn't want to reap it
I didn't sow it
because I knew the moment I said it
the words would come find me
so I swallowed them
never told a soul
how much I came to rue
the truth I always knew
not every man who comes for your hand
comes for your heart

Along Came You

Along came you
A certain well-built dapper you
an oh-so-gorgeous you
You must have smelled the extremity in me
the desperation I bled
Along came you with the deep-brown eyes
lost in them, another world to me
One glance
Your visage was unparalleled to any human before me
You were not the first to immorally request
but you are the first to affectionately advance
The look of you struck me
I hung on your words lovely
your compliments puffed me
The baddest chick in the industry had nothing on me
your words made me feel like a necessity
you gave me just what I craved
Paid attention to my technicalities
Doled out enough ear candy
to anesthetize the desolate malady
caused by the others delinquency
I will resist you fervently
armor up carefully
deny any manner of unity
and dismiss you immediately
But then you kissed me…
The nuptial agreement—broken instantly

Eye to Eye I (Before Climax)

Your voice said
my heart speaks
and we accept
dance the dance
with spoken word
speaking to flesh
meet me there
ask me again
tell me where
take my word
send me there
you talk to me
like fresh air
finish me
my word can't bear
complete me
the thoughts...unique
look into this—unity
no one to understand
tango with chance
these words: not happenstance
good words, hard words
f**k me words
like this, like that kinda words
stir me up inside words,

ignite me words
wet words…lift me
already there
reach me there
yea…right there
say the word
I am ready to hear
do not depart
singe into my heart
these lips speak of real things
heavy parts
contain them here
dare not release these words
into the air
the quiet ear…can hear
resounding fear
impending…keep it near
speak not again
your voice said
my mind said
our bodies said
eye to eye
let's keep this
it is our own
deny it all
no one will ever know
what was meant
it wasn't spoken
mouths closed

Time finds me alone where
elaborate thoughts take space and ruminate
I look like one living in normalcy
but quietly, I contemplate
everything

There are things I believe to be beyond me
cause I was raised better than…right?
things other women can be
words outside of my reach
these thoughts taking life in me
someone's religion keeps me in my place
but temptation…
I continue, I contemplate

Caught up in immaterial things
the unreal sensation of things not yet seen or heard
how is it possible that my heart has run away from me?
run away from this house
these walls, these sheets…
because I let another one in my emotional blood stream
arduously, I'm chasing after me
clandestinely, I entertain my secret
he is the one I wish to captivate
for it would seem he has come to fascinate
every need fallen by another's wayside
and try hard in my might
to flee, it is to he
I want to fall away toward

Dialogue in the Dark

loneliness talks to me
lust whispers in me
regret talks to me
contempt talks to me
fear talks at me
intention talks to me
boredom talks to me
risk bribes me
curiosity talks to me
opportunity beckons me
trepidation warns me
anticipation calls to me
my conscience shouts at me
the dark talks to me
the light tells me
spirit murmurs in me
God, do you hear me?

Eye to Eye II (After Climax)

Receive me
I am your quest
honor me
chill, be easy
look into me...kiss me
your lips, your tongue
I want to suck you
choke you
opening
what is this feeling
intensity
hungry energy
redirect
hold me
undulating
purrrrrr baby...into me
opening wider
she is speaking; my body
are you hearing
you answer
I resist — you persist
like electricity
soft shocks
up and down
my back...my side
wider, don't...open me

and you search me
find in me
a special unknown
admit defeat
I want you in me
it is all too deep
surrender me
tender love-like
complicating the banal life
cleave to me, connect with me
seize me!
not to f**k me, maybe slightly
introduce your love to me
into me let it see
your eyes are endless
they make me want more
I cry for me
give my tears release
accept me, console me
play with me
break the rules
too many words
precious
keep hold of me
not to be shared
there is a calm here
no pain here
inevitably must leave here
something remains…while I go
I lick my lips
I remember you

Moment of Weakness

Experiencing a moment of weakness
wanting to run away
wanting to step outside of myself
and rush to meet me at the end
The end where it's all said and done
the end where every...thing is in the open
the end where who remains—does
All uttered and exhausted
all exposed
all weight cast down
all the confusion smothered
all the turmoil finished
all the dis-ease released
All the you should, you could, silenced
all the tears wiped away, dried up
all the falsehood, past

This is where I am in thought
but not where I am in body
in this hour, I am weary
I am tired
I am ready...to give up
At this particular moment
glass eyes, hurt heart
not knowing what to do

not wanting to do the wrong do
the easy do
the run-away-from-this-just-to-be do
I need one moment of clarity
one moment in this time continuum
where nothing is about me
One clear moment; no juggling
the emotions of three
he…she…he…
one damn moment with only me
I want to run away to a place called peace

Pause…allow my face to leak
This is what one does in that moment
where one feels weak

Interlude

I bit into the flesh of him with everything I had
took in his milky sweetness
his sticky goodness
like a baby savoring the succor of a breast
I consumed him until his poison numbed my tongue
blackened my teeth
and left me for dead
I tasted no evil in him
yet he stole my soul, snatched my breath
I'm wandering lost without him
hungry for something I have never had
my fear, I will be left
incapable of ever sinking into another again

Again and Again

I run with intensity
only to walk back in humility
I reason with self furiously
losing a winning battle overtly
I tell myself again and again
you're no good for me
it's not pride
it is curiosity that makes me return continually

My laughter had gone
my energy depleted
today I live in your song,
feeling completed
I hold on tightly
I let go lightly
but lyrics of me looking sightly
make me desire you nightly

Again and again
I invite your invasion
of my mind, my heart, my body
oh, the sensation
I love how we make happy
and make naughty then nice
the sweet nothing of everyday together

is my vice
dreading an end in calamity

It is the power of the sentient being in me
and so I persist in a wrestle
in my mind, with my heart
knowing while we exhilarate together
we should suffer aloneness apart
I often wonder how our story ends
or when it begins
Time will yield the expectations within

Becoming Love

morning tea and evening coffee
it was in the way he adored
her ways and served her ardently
when he came to be; I love you

her tonic of spring sentiment
him devoted to her soft strength
devoted to her heart's ballad
as he came to be; I love you

he threatened to love her with more
than elegant words, but with deeds
with mum prayers and covenant rings
yes, he came to be; I love you

she wasn't perfect when he came
and he begged her never to be
she believed he loved, so he did
and he came to be; I love you

More

This is what you do in me...

In life we encounter people,
live, breathe and break bread with them
and still never know
the whispers in them
surrounded by empty organisms,
we become familiar strangers
all Earth-intruders occupying Mars and Venus
You inspire me to live on Earth
to grow and to know you
to be true to me and you
to be myself and allow you
to embrace the equation: us
basking in the sun...light-en us
You arouse me to be love: uninhibited
grow love: naturally
and gift love: in its purest form
for Our Higher Being
in all our human moments accumulated
imagining the us yet to happen keeps me lifted
so high
two living beings just being
there are far more galaxies to occupy
but on Earth, I choose to reside beside you

let us not waste or dilute our human existence
More to reach, the stars, they align
Heaven and Earth agree

Love,
you've stained my heart
with ambiguous inkblots
resembling no human I've blamed on you

And Love,
every time I think I will know you
I am bludgeoned by a stark sensibility
you will not conform for me...

Love, I'm on a mission to be familiar with you
really experience you
You see,
I've searched for you inside layers of skin
pressing bodies
holding hands
but you reside not in fingerprints

I find, I am most apprehended when
there is none but you and me
in the cool of a room
in the darkest dim
and in sheer silence you speak
and from pages of sages, words leap
causing a yearning to gallop in me

But Love,
when shall I know you in the shape of a heartbeat
in the form of a man outside of me
because I'm afraid

and although you tell me not to be
I lack confidence in the mortals near to me

Alas, Love,
you've stained me
marked me untouchable territory
from what do you save me for?

Intermission

It was falling leaves
an array of cayenne reds and burnt oranges
and amber yellows twirling
whipping through the brisk

The sun kissed the left side of my face
touched the corner of my smile
a warmth felt me
in the magic of autumn's equinox

It will be cold soon
leaning into the season of my life

Sweet Misery

Misnomered Sweet Misery
when so in love with her company
She desired one to commiserate
rather, one does placate
Dare admit the source found in her does satiate

And though she slays one with words
One will yet trust her, lust for her
and gird oneself from unfeigned truth heard
In this quest, she still does err

Removing layers of decay
resulted from deprivation
entering into a far away
At the door please stay your intimidation
your apprehension,
New is good when openly received and understood

Pseudonym Sweet Misery
because ultimate goal is sincerity
into me I want one to see
intimacy in its purest form
realize one can't match her exactitude
Uncommon, rare, study this beatitude

Placed in one's hand—for purpose
Question not the plan—remain with focus
Hold captive the presence of her
before the scent of her
lingers...
leaving misery to the company
she keeps not
to caress heavy emptiness in one's fingers

Too much has furthered;
running fast to nowhere when still much is left
to begot

Sobriquet Sweet Misery
not accidentally,
fortuitously by design
enchanted
Misery does love one's company
as one's company desires her misery
intoxicating curiosity, refined sensuality
Continue to commiserate,
surreptitiously partake
rapture once found is hard to escape

Silly of Me

I believed
without words
tacitly
but with body
agreed,
conjugated a fidelity
to what degree...

Silly of me to desire loyalty, expect integrity,
when I step outside in secrecy
indecently
to expose myself to he
with whom I forsook my vows
a he who did not belong to me

and you deny me
the honor of your truth
I thought there was nothing to hide from me
because I hid behind you

a tattered ticket stub
proof embodied
I am not the only one who lies with lies...
your special moments don't all belong to me
it's just that I allowed myself to believe

falsely
that I was your one and only
special sin

silly of me to request from you
that which I snatched from the first he...

so I find the things we hide
crawl inside until we pull them out
show them to the light
where they either flourish
or fall and die

hold no secrets in; they fall out

Judgment Day

I
with a judgmental judge
and strangers as jury
I wished God's voice could have defended me
but it felt more like
He left me alone
to fend on my own
have I been forsaken…
Lord, are you mad at me?

II
sat in the courtroom beside me
I was guilty of sin
adultery
she took my scarlet letter

peeled the shame off me
scattered it away
as far as the west is from the east
I haven't seen shame since

poured a tall glass of wine for me
the night before the sentencing
we drank in silence

she was loud and clear

interceded for me
when I went in
made the life sentence
a little easier
to breathe

gave me permission
to taste my tears
let them rinse my flaws
let them make me soft

never asked questions
she's my hide-the-body friend
the one to remind me:
no condemnation

her loyalty: absolute
and her kindness: priceless
perhaps God borrowed her body
to be flesh with me

Interlude

I never loved him righteously,
I discounted his love,
kept record of his wrongs,
deemed him unworthy
because the truth is
I didn't believe I was worthy
and the truth will always be
from your body to any body
you will never give
what you do not have already
harvested within

I Had It Coming

I had a healing to transfer
I really didn't mean to hurt you, sir
but a beating I suffered
assault and battery was what he gave to me
like I earned the penalty
of manly fists pounding the side of me
filled with indignation
rage engulfed quietly in his rib cage
penetrated as his blows reverberated
against the *graceful* body
of the woman he once joined in ceremony
every offence to his psyche
every trespass I tallied
he transferred back to me
as he took his time to pummel me
hardwood floors bracing me

I could not have expected
to abscond with my transgression
a sorry religious convection
this my comeuppance

still cognizant enough to beg and plead
for the episode to cease in peace
for one call to the authorities

would alter the lives of three tragically
so I took it, I let him beat me
acquiesce…
let him exact revenge on me
b/c to lose my children would be the true
irreversible injury
and when Husband was done and departed into the night
I nursed the battered body
and lay with my children beside me
their little bodies holding me tight

And the next day…
at Lover's house
upon arrival, he kissed my blackened eyes
and politely f**ked me
that is how he honored me
there was nothing left to defend in me

to have to persuade the mind of
and assuage the hands
of your attacker

to have to expose
exhausted emotions
to temper
your tormentor

this is the place I am within

to have to proclaim blame
as if I chose it

to have to allay them
because eyes that see
believe the chauvinism they learned
and according to them
this I deserved

this is the place I am found within

to have to be in the adultering body
carrying a guilty conscience
playing with free will
dancing with insanity

this is my within

Interlude

I promise not to wear grief as a warm sweater
Nor regret like comfortable shoes
Rather, I will let peace adorn me and joy rest in my heart
I allow miracles to run me over
and chase me into faithful fields where love takes care of all
I allow miracles to run me over
and lay me upon still waters where grace washes it all
away…

Ego Tripping

Ego tripping
who's slipping?
pride then fall
We slip and fall into bouts of silence
Is this what it feels like to sleep with the devil...?

In the quiet time I am
exposed in veiled truths
sensational thoughts, feelings
over fraudulent reasons
But really, what is the meaning?
what am I fearing?
complicating the simplest form of being
competing to further dehydrate the sound of healing
a fast from speaking
again, I ask for the true meaning
behind our silent feuding

We feed our front with pride
quell our ego with insolence
shooting blanks
we are empty
so chary of explanation
consequently
two hearts apart

when really needing to protect
our chambers, our sacrosanct
presiding under the same sky
our skulls deluded in residue
one basic question reigns:
When do I speak to you?

Because with each passing hour
another dose of girl power
no more delicate flower
We are evaporating
you disappoint me......
I disappoint you
Will we ever reach the apogee?
I should say a eulogy...

I want to throw away the feelings you threw my way
I should have never caught them
I'd like to say you won't catch me again
I'm discarding *hue*—
all your mixed up colors and shades of blue
fade me out from the memory of you

Silence broken
pride fallen
every time you come callin'
I go runnin'...
a sinner running to her coffin

Maybe it is the way he does the little things
something like the little things that say I care for you
like maybe it is the way he runs my temperate bath water
and settles me down with a chill glass of wine
Or maybe it is the way he gingerly, tenderly washes me up
with his soft touch
and other times it is the way he kisses my forehead,
my shoulder, endearing
He has me under emotional arrest
it is his way of making me stay
And when his fingers strum me a tune
I get lost in the adagios of him
And I know it is in the way he looks at me
with his bedroom brown eyes
those eyes I want to believe even as they lie
because it is the way he would lay his hand on my lap
on the ride to any store, any place
sitting beside me, adding to the hold on me
Or the way he would place his palm on the nape of
my neck
assuring me
And it is the way that he would stand over me
I want to look up to him
It is all his ways
the way that his hands cut my fruit,
peel my vegetables
the way that his hands serve me
Or the way he makes my coffee
just the way I like it
so much cream, so much sugar

he is so sweet when he wants to be
Oh yes, it was and is the way he enters in
and around
up and down
my entire body
It is his way of keeping me under carnal arrest
emotional duress
lost in our flesh
It is his sex
that keeps me coming back

Woe Is Not Me

I find myself
curled up in the distant details of what was
nowhere near the meticulous matter of what is
slipping under what I indulge to deny
don't want to be
in self-pity
a lulling loneliness
and sometimes even in the most excruciating
monotonous moments
of living and having my being
I am captured by a brief interval in the dawn
to find myself
slipping under Aurora's phenomenon
in a field of lavender and eucalyptus
and the shades of my life
are not so despisable and unwanted after all
because the good and the bad and the lovely
all work together
to send me
along the passion purposed for
the exclusively
complicated uncommon me

still learning to settle into my extraordinary destiny

Aphonia

Shame on me
I fell in love with the words inside his mouth
he wouldn't speak
cause a father told him
it wasn't macho to release need and want to a lady
So I suck on his tongue to hear him
And when he sips on fine wine
I taste the flavor of his dark Merlot heart
though I'd prefer a sweet whiskey
If only he would say those words I need to hear
then I wouldn't kiss him so much...
I wouldn't linger so long
waiting on his mouth to utter
what already his heart told me

Or do I just hear an echo in me...

Wanting, Needing, Never Again

It's not that I don't want to call you,
cause I do
want to call you,
invite you over to sit down under a cloud
watch the sky cry
but I fear you'll make me pour just as bad
right after you've bent me over to worship my moon…
you have a way of reminding me
I'm not the brightest star in your sky leading you home

It's not that I don't want to call you
because I do
for nothing in particular and everything particular
so I could watch you watch me
feel you feel me
on a bed of roses and daisies
awaiting you to deflower me
pluck my petals–he loves me, he loves me not…enough

I want to call you, but I won't
I can accept you won't give me the love I give
But I need the love I need
anything less would be betrayal to me
so I'll fight not to call you,
deny the wanting of you
repent the human games we play
cause underneath it all, there is a love choking

Interlude

This morning summer departed
leaving only a familiar sun ray
to remind me
Startled by cold sheets against my body
I'd rather your warmth jostling my hungry...
to a hidden bird chirping in the distance
between us and the world
I crave you out there
the way you run your course in my veins
heat leaving me
temperature rising
your summer falling on me
Our season changing

So that I might remember
that there are nights
when we can be still enough
that touch reminds us that we are not
strangers in the heart
So that I can remember
that I could contain you
and fill you up with
all the love that lives inside of me
that I could overflow in the hold of you
So that I remember
I give you tears of undeniable joy in the
crux of our obscure pain
that you could be nothing and everything
to me in one breath
You continue to confound me
and love survives us continually

Love Bleed

Dearly beloved
the things your mouth did say
I believed the words in you
you insult me with your wordplay
profess hard-core infinite no-limit love
with your voice
while you lay in the middle of me
nestled between my thighs
begging me to let you in…
tempting choice
you pulsate on me,
syncopating with my heartbeat
circling my hymen,
I want to swallow you, devour you
I believe the words you pour into me
manipulate my thoughts, my emotions
with your false tongue
just to cum freely
bathe me sticky

You've trained your embrace well to emulate safety
my God, you hurt me
I cry uncontrollably
I look into your deep-brown eyes
even them you've trained in the art of illusory

who taught you such trickery
to dishonor and deceive me
with your being, your body
your living trumps all the wisdom I thought to have in me
your words speak of longevity and momentary eternity
all in the aim of ejaculating profusely
your hot lava into my hungry pussy
on my stomach, on my chest,
breathing hot and heavy, over my breast

I'm starved of love with you
my insides want to envelope your thrust
and choke your lust
until you fall limp inside
and slowly slide out from between my sweaty thighs
warmness slowly drizzling out
wetness quenching my drought
to leave a cold puddle
on my bed
for wise woman sense to return
when you rear your head
my heart becomes heavy
reality is deafening
because your silence is awakening
all the doubt revolting in me
a civil war boiling in me
so, in this reality I will not surrender my body
or the remnant of virtue
that still courses in me

You've denied love long enough
no need to improvise another lie
no need to fake a false eternity
no need to finger or penetrate my red royalty
I want to hate you for such travesty
but hurt is more prevalent, honestly
so I close me—no honorary intimacy
I must live to fade you from memory
for tacitly, you told me
I am not worthy of anything holy
so leave me in dignity
naked clothed in His security
sometimes the right choice feels so wrong
cause the wrong phallus feels so right
but, no illusion
this is our final concrete conclusion

Interlude

but you reject me
make me wrong
for wanting to love
all your wretched beauty
the intricates that christened you human
you were always precious to me
you were always worth loving to me
loving the beauty of you with the rest of you
has been my hardest test

when you find the voice to confess
when you find the heart to break
when you find the courage to be weak
when you can stand to fall in this love

only…

when you give the love I need
when you can give the love you have
when you can love the way we are
then will you have me near
dear, have me to hold
for as long as your breath and body can live for me

only…

then

then only will I give to you all of me

Down This Road

Memory one
memory two
sitting alone, writing my sad song
fighting tears,
I've been here before
inundated with dead thoughts
ghost memories
the exchange of eyes
the exchange of smiles
numbers, time, conversation
emotions, changes, time,
essence, bodies, privates, solitudes
the transfer of fears, more emotions
volitional, unconsciousness
movements, time, relapses
the exchange of plans, dreams, affections
future memories
the exchange of me onto you
so many exchanges
then change to ex
Exit from my life
exchange of belongings
sorry apologies
tired tears, exhausted energy, dirty laundry
changed to ex

exhibitions of fears, trepidations
wayward waves, ups and down
ambivalence
arounds, falling deeper into a familiar comfort-
able discomfort

Exchanged heartbeats and pulses
now I am concrete, solid
facing the facts
my palms are empty
I did hold you steady, fonder, too near to me
expound, could never to me
I occupied spaces and words you would never see
Love, that was your abnormality
didn't have it to give
couldn't take it
violently allergic to it
you couldn't receive, did you ever believe
couldn't conceive that you could contain
what He gave us to free
you held it tight, prisoner
retrieve
And I am still withholding
the cleansing of the eyes
the baptizing of the heart
the purging of the mind
We shall struggle no more, no longer
each other removed from our beings
two solitudes released from hazard
from the clutch of purgatory

Go and be, grow and be

And please, allow the free flow to clearly see
must grieve the time I gave for
it will never be returned to me
the effort I gave
the energy I gave
the loyalty I gave
the support I gave
the encouragement I gave
the understanding I gave
the everything I gave
the forgiveness I extended
the truths I blinded
the memories I amended
the affection I lended
the nucleus I rended
the body I offered
the lady I martyred
the inside I sacrificed
the I, I divided
the too much I rendered
it is finished now

Now is here
and here is not there, or where it could have been
or never went, never was
this is the beginning of an end
to anew end
start fresh then

begin new, remain true
release negative energy
breath into positivity
acquire new vocabulary
focus on primary
celebrate solidarity

Not mourning what could have been
and never was
not mourning the chances we took
not mourning the voices ignored, unheeded
not mourning the should have, could have walked away
not mourning the couldn't take me as I am, as we are, as
we will be
not mourning you are not for me
not mourning your loss, for I am found
not mourning
Waiting for morning
and I pray that when I lay down to rest
I do not lose slumber, fret or stray from
the peace I am channeling
Letting it Go

I don't need to prolong this anymore
I don't need to talk about it anymore
I don't need to lose over this anymore
I don't need this anymore
Because there is more
there is more to live for
more to grow for

more to sing, dance and laugh for
more to love
there is more, there is greater
asking only to unite with it
become with it
the More
because I deserve it
I am more
And more deserves, desires and beseeches for me
More finds me
A kindred spirit is around the bend
I Am Well.

Intermission

Dust to dust
When too much of nothing becomes something
when all the dead weight begins to amass and accumulate
imposing as living...
I take to the clouds
Flutter my wings softly and transcend
peek down to observe the rushing
the mindless travel of frantic mortals
giving away time to unimportant matters
that will always remain on Earth even as we rise to heaven
the moral of today's story
none of this is real...enough
it is all dust, blow it away

Time doesn't always heal;
it simply fades away
the daily ailments
dressed up as letting go
costumed as forgetting
little white lying
denying
we are always desiring
conspiring…
for a sugar-coated night
still needing nakedness
still secretly praying for an alone
a one more together

Out of Breath

So why don't you
go ahead and say everything you need to say
all the rehearsed thoughts
all the memorized lines
you keep running and rewriting in your head
because I feel them

All the things you haven't said…
they've already leaked out of you
your actions have become so loud
I'm tone-deaf to you
So go ahead and say all that's true
because the day is young still
and we are getting old,
not wise

You should let me
look into you
let me see the vulnerability that binds you
let me un-sew the fibers that make you
Because the truth of our matter is
all you have is now
For tomorrow I die
knowing nothing of the words locked in your heart
feeling none of the soft words in your hand

asphyxiated in the silence
I die knowing only the void of our distance
rubbing the callous of our failed love

Tonight an angel holds me
tomorrow I will ascend into a vast sky never reaching our
highest high
Because pride
you kept yourself from me, waiting for tomorrow
Because hurt
you held love from me, waiting until next week
Because trust
you rest well with our grudge…
Because your wounds eclipse me

Your morning is promised
but Heaven forbid
you lose every opening to behold me
in this lifetime
Heaven forbid
never is when you'll have the moment again
Let Heaven forbid
you miss me while I'm alive
only to remember me when I'm dead

So go ahead
with all the new moon magic you can summon in you
never mind the sun
But now
tell me what you want to do
with this one life you still have gasping in me

Intermission

And if you should happen to
walk into sadness under the sunshine
know that the sun cries too
it finds solace in the clouds
and thanks the moon

And if you should happen to
lose faith in who you are
talk to the sky
talk to the breeze
talk to any natural thing
beautiful and bigger than you

And if you should happen to
fall weak in your strength
darling, take a deep breath
hum a long song
and let the groans of your heart
speak to your God
just let yourself be
all the convoluted, non-simple, sporadic, emotional
feelings you want to be

Because it isn't
if you should happen to
But because
you will

Bird's Song

I'll be honest.
It's because of you I hear the bird's song in the morning.
I remember the first time we heard a sunny
serenade together.
We were still. We were aware. We were fragile. Opened
in love.
Now, we are no more and much less…
Distilled humans, cradling black and white memories.
And now, every time I hear them sing,
I remember, you were the first one who gave me
their sweet songs in the morning.

Wisdom...

Young girl growing up,
Daddy told me
it was my burden
to earn the love of the man
who came for me
and after over-doing, over-giving
over-staying and over-compensating...
Today, young girl, grown lover
I know I deserve his love...free
not something to barter or reap,
and not at the cost of my integrity
but a love ripened long before the
expectation of me

Interlude

I still feel a great deal. But
I don't pray for Him to take
the bitter cup from me. I drink.
Dredge and all...Because
I've learned how important it is.
To drink from misery.
It is the harmony of a light head
and heavy heart that drags,
my impatient body
to an abiding sobriety.

Pass Bye...Familiar Stranger

The unknowing naked eye would notice nothing:
person A, person B,
lost in a crowded people sea
passing bye

If one passed us by,
they would never know,
how familiar the strangers are,
it is this act that is foreign to us

If she saw me pass him by,
she would never know
that once upon a time he was my guy, my armor
we didn't shine in the masses
but heart did kindle quietly upon sight

If he saw him pass me by,
he would never know
there were nights when I unraveled him,
when he pumped me full with adrenaline pearls,
produced sound as he tracked,
loved as we slumbered

Countless nights into days we spent
like radio heads lost in a wordless chorus

found in cinematic orchestras
Locked away, hidden from the world

But if you passed us by today,
you wouldn't hear heart palpitations,
or thoughts hidden in trepidation,
you wouldn't see heart contusions,
or vituperous incisions
sharp words like knives cut deep,
sever arteries, puncture lungs, drain body…
I bleed no more: coagulated

Now we are trained,
to deceive the masses and lie to the heart
falsify evidence, suffer ignominy—my part
and pass by the walking dead
nothing remains to resuscitate,
unapologetic, for sorry is a condition not a correction
it cannot erase or ameliorate

Today, the unknowing eye will only ever see:
person A, person B
blended among a people sea,
random third parties
passing bye

I think I miss the memory of you more than the real you
I sat in the presence of tangible you, touchable you...
blue...
When I'm awake, I can't believe our dreams will come true
But you, now you do, said you won't try, but will do...
All the things required to make we a brighter hue...
So, I'll hold my hope, anticipate our better, a life anew...

Intermission

the sun came looking for you this morning
while you yet rested
she waited with a quiet excitement
with more than a handful of light
to pour golden into your eyes, upon your skin
to pour her passion into your resting heart
the sun came looking for you this morning
there is no hiding from her warmth
extend your arms and let life embrace you
did you know the new day comes to love you?

How I imagine God would talk to me

He is near to Her,
for he cannot stay away too long
for him, she is home

Her body is peace…
for the blues in him
cannot be without her jazz

On a melancholy Sunday morning
the sweet in his sorrow
is in Her sanctuary

Just for Tonight Because
I'll Be Gone in the Morning

So just
lay me down
on a sheet marked of words you've never said
let me feel their coldness under my back
as I lay on your bed
speak them close to me
so that the sound of them remains in my head
remains in my head
remains in my head

That you'd rather us dead
than to breathe again
that you'd rather us dead
than to chance again
that you'd rather us play dead
than to live again

Lay my body down on your empty bed
and shed
your old skin, your old ways, your old song
all of your oldness
and maybe cover me with a new you
lay me down
and wake me up in the morning

before the alarm rings
before reality stings
and your lies become living things
crawling…

Catch me
maybe while I'm still drifting on the wings
of dawn
just lay with me as I come to
from sleep
you don't have to speak…

If only for this night
because I don't want to rise
in your morning

Cause the issues of my heart
always fall out of my mouth
when his stream of consciousness
flows through my body

In the Beginning...

In the beginning, you desired me
It was a sweet beginning when you cherished me,
breathed to adore me
when you opened heart and doors for me
prepared body and table to receive me
anticipated the aura that summed me

In the beginning, you were prompted to love me
In the beginning, you would not expire on me
you diligently pursued me exclusively–gently
forbidden fruit is so sweet when relished clandestinely

In the beginning, you gave words and songs to me
poured visions of the life you seek into me
In the beginning, I was a delight, a treasure kept from sight
a marvel, I would be consumed
There was no power enough to deny us room
In the beginning I was the prize, the present was me

Fine-tuning: it was always illusory
for bittersweet granted became all of me
I aspired to go the way with you
down so many paths
When I am still, I think of you
going through the math

the increments of incidents and moments ignored–
the math became too much
When I began to lose count of the offenses on my
own hands
the times I counted on your fingers…
was when I should have about faced and went along
my merry way
but every time I counted backwards
I found one more reason to stay
Your memory brings a knowing to me
of living long gone and life to come
In the beginning: this is past
those things from our beginning: they didn't last

With each new beginning, I gain with different day
I real-eyes our ending was postponed by my fervent ways
I realize I miss you–but will persist away
I, looking with clear eyes, see the new beginning
the memories of you that come to visit
are passages of time that will soon be distant
My memories are the making of you, the severing from
you
at times the illuminating of you, the sincere praying
for you
but really the missing of you, and the slow steady fading of
you
from the beginning

I won't have it
if I don't trust me

and I don't deserve it
if I don't have it in me

to our end
accept it from me

I can love you because
I love me

Abandon-Her

Because I've come to know you as someone who leaves me
we could be together and loneliness impended me;
Our smiles and laughter, short-lived, because you left and
didn't take me with you
not the whole me, but the most revered part of me
you could have tucked in your breast pocket,
that would have been enough for me
I could never enjoy the midst of us, the thing that other
people saw at the mere sight of we,
because they don't know that you use me, contuse me,
than leave me

And in the moments of our togetherness,
I would grip you with all that I was, all that I am, just to
keep you with me
because the moment was always upon me,
waiting for the minute you would leave me
and not leave me like, okay, I'll see you later, baby
or okay, I'll call you when I get home, my lady
but immanently leave me
because it was trending,
you were more and more not there for me
you didn't belong to me and maybe too, that's what it is
that I always wanted you to belong to me
but you never would

and you would always leave me in the knowing
I am alone without you
Concealing me, refusing to claim me,
all the more suppressing the essence of me in you

Being with your cold reality, you are not for me
each time you left through my door was a subtle
devastation
of what it would look like
of what life would be like without the smell of
your cologne
lingering
because I knew I could not count on you on all my fingers
still hooked on a mirage of you, reflected when first I
saw you
fell for you, more and more illusory is the man I met when
I first acquainted with you
the two faced man who knew, just what to say and do
Jekyll or Hyde, after all this time
not knowing me nor caring enough to say, I got home,
sweetie
it's all good I love you, baby
I never got I love you because you didn't love me

I had to train myself to be okay with not saying I love you
I had to train myself to not end our phone calls with I love
you
I had to train myself to not end our time with I love you
I had to train myself not to love you
You did that;

that's what you gave me
because you could never seal our occasions with I love you

But who am I lying to?
All my training never quenched the love I grew for you
Just as all my training never grew a genuine I love you to
the one before you

Interlude

Because love must be tested
for it to be real
It must endure
at least one trial—hung jury
and some several tribulations
It must suffer through seasons
dried up leaves and precipitation
Fall apart to come together again
Because if we don't make it through…
then it was never real love to begin with

Nothing but the Fool

thorny like the roses you picked
just to calm me
down
under…
your kiss tastes like promise
your touch feels like "I do"
want
so much more than…
you elude me
and the diamonds in your eyes
avoid my ring finger
I'm over the long lasting short whiles
I'd prefer a moment of forever with you
nothing but the fool in me
keeps letting you
render me…
broken like the flowers
you picked
just to calm me down
because
we both know
you'll never ask me to I do

Intermission

Mother Earth is writing a poem
with falling tears
She writes of a sunrise lost in the morning after the storm
She mourns her light in the moment
washes her soul and waits for inspiration to unfold from
the ground
The trees will know the sun again
and she will know joy once more

In Surrender

I choose no more attempts
to make peace or break silence
I'm staying in the stillness
of nothing…
where I find goodness
I am tired of wrestling in my within
I am sullen in my womb
because our nature doesn't progress for unity
constantly warring
we are quick to remove ourselves
and advance…
sadly towards lonely selves
we never escape our fragile selves
we leave short of value time after time
to start over again
from nowhere
this is our shame
there is no beauty about us

but if I stay in my peace
sedated in a safe space…
I remember to heal
not bury and forget

The Truth, the Fantasy, the Reality

Truth:
Every time the clock strikes 8:50, I think of you
Every time I have a cup of coffee sweetened with hazelnut,
I taste you
Every time I hear good music, I feel you

Fantasy:
Every time I miss a call, I wanna see your number
Every time I've had a long day, I wanna see your face
Every time I lay me down, I wanna see your eyes

Reality:
Every time I have hope, you disappoint me
Every time I need you most, you abandon me
Every time I hold you close, you deceive me

Truth:
Every time I hear your name, I get a feeling
Every time I go to work, I think, will I see him?
Every time I go to church, I remember you

Fantasy:
Every time I'm lost, I wanna find you
Every time I drink, I miss you

Every time I get horny, I wanna ride you

Reality:
Every time I give you a chance, you play me
Every time I believe in you, you make a fool of me
Every time you give me your word, I doubt me
Every time you said you got it, you didn't
Every time you said you meant it, you didn't
Every time I lamented, you didn't

More Reality:
Every time I let you in, I'm left with out
Every time I move on, you creep back in
Every time I say no more, you plead once again

Truth:
Every time I'm done writing about you, you give my words
more hue
Every time I'm done with the subject of you, history
repeats itself in full view
Every time I waste etymology on you, I memorialize you

So this time, you found your way, but didn't get in
This time, you pleaded I changed, but
couldn't demonstrate
This time, I played my cards right, and your hand fell apart
This time, you didn't get your thing wet, so now you upset
This time, you did exactly what you did last time,
no surprise
This time, I still had hope, but blank expectations

This time, and every time you remain exactly who
you've been…
The truth hurts, cold reality, f**k a fantasy!

Truth & Reality:
But this time, I didn't allow you in me, through me or
around me
But this time, I believe you don't deserve me
But this time, I know you know, you lost me
But this time, I didn't ignore the knowledge in me
But this time, I remained loyal to the wisdom in me
But this time, I love more the woman I be

Interlude

If we weren't so empty inside
we wouldn't be so reckless
with filling ourselves

let me count the ways I filled up…
only to remain empty

desiring full-fillment

Intermission

A breeze brushes the evergreen
a spider spins her silk
the pond glitters of rustic gold
and just beyond the tracks
over a graffiti-ridden train
fluttering wings soar high

Suspended in the calm of it all
taking in the seasoned Spring
on a still, sky-blue Saturday
Evening holds on to Sun for a little longer
but soon she'll make way for the Stars
and the sky will dance to the tune of the Moon

Karma

I can't wait for karma to catch up with you
years from now, when I'm chronologically behind you
years later, when enough time and distance has anesthe-
tized you
faded my fragrance from the scent of you
make vintage the wine you once imbued
more time and distance for new memories
before the senescence settles in
life enough to help you forget
your acts of commission and sins of omission

I want karma to find you in the form of a man
richer than you, more gorgeous than you, slimmer
than you,
so much fresher than you, with the gumption to
introduce himself into your play-it-safe life
impersonate your role without strife
and steal your young, beautiful wife
from your stained hands; they're dirty
there is still dried blood under your fingernails

I want you to fall short
so that she can look up to him tall
I want him to suffuse your space
and permeate your place

ravage her body
penetrate her mind
breach her essence
I want him to burglarize any remnant of you from
her temple
He will become the altar to which she sacrifices you

I want this for you
so you can taste what sweet misery you put
another through
I want this for you
knowing your backbone is not strong enough to sup-
port you
knowing that your pride will precede your tumultuous fall

You have no substance at all
to endure what you sentenced another to
I want karma to sink its teeth in you
draw blue blood, saline tears, realize all your fears
Drain mortal breath from you
to leave you marked with a scarlet letter
Reading this of you:

I am a man who lies, cheats and destroys
for my menial pleasures
I have no intentions to be your forever man
Could care less about the plunder of precious treasures
And for your future, I have a reckless plan
Could not care much for the hurt I dole out
beyond measure

I will play the part of your number one fan
But know this: my only aim is to please my pleasure,
And under any pressure, I will abandon you to stand
Alone in your hell

You are the bane of my existence
I, *prey*…you rue the day…
may karma consume you satiably
sate my hunger for vengeance
and excrete you from its body like you did me
You must regret the trespasses you did to me
May that young perfect wife
kill your pride, your manhood, your dignity
ever so subtly

May your penitence drag slowly
May karma swallow you wholly
and when it does, because it will
don't call me…
I already know the end
karma showed me

Thou Shall Not Kiss Me & Curse Me with the Same Mouth

Because somehow through the shifting of clouds
and the fulling of moons
and all the seasons our reasons have been through

It became acceptable for one mouth
to say I love you, so let me hurt you
Acceptable for our lover's one mouth
to profess I adore you and spit debasement and pro-
lific abuse

It's become too okay;
in fact too cliché
for our lover's one mouth to kiss us ever so tender
and curse us till we are rendered
fragile and broken becomings...

So, while we are being, learning and loving
my only one commandment remains standing
Thou shall not kiss me and curse me with the same mouth

Because, darling,
those are not the words I want to taste
less I regurgitate...them...on you...
Rather, give me something sweet to lick off my lips

every time we kiss;
every time we stand face to face
feed me words to live within
And for our sake,
as we endeavor from day to day
speak the words that help love stay

The life we make together;
let it begin and end with abiding Love

When Words Collide

in the foot of my mouth is a quart of moonshine
I'm gulping for courage to say a few words to you
I'd write them down,
but then I'd have to see them outside of myself
I'm not ready to read a spilling of the ironies
and reveries between us two
and all the ways we almost never made it
hindsight is 20/20, but I'm still blind
as to how we moved around the elephant in the room

in the back of my throat
a lot of innocent words lodged
and details the devil plays chess with
I never seem to make the right move
I thought you would see me through the chapters of
my story
all these pages, dog-eared holding a few words
I'd like to say to you
which one is your favorite–oh I forget
I ripped out a sheet
the one that recounts the home in my heart
in past tense
now vacant dilapidated

but I'd rather put my foot in my mouth
than to repeat what I said yesterday
or the day before
there are no new words left to speak
for the same old thing you give me
in the foot of my mouth,
a pile of dust
I'm coughing up

your resentment lingers in
me
like black tea steeped,
sugar-coated as cotton candy
sticky
like sweet love trickling
warm milk,
slippery
I've tripped, fallen hard
tangled in a bad case of you
still trying to figure out
what my soul looks like
free of your residue
I've got to get the ghost of you
out of me

Choose Me

said you prefer that I come without my armor
yet at the first sight of bare chest,
you trampled the heart
beneath my breast

and what it was always about
is that you would choose me
over and over and over…daily
not maybe
because there would always stand an opportunity
for you to choose me…artfully
like I was your muse

choose me, over pride
choose me, over fear
choose me, over the facade
choose me from the left side of your brain
over the doubts, over the appearance of things
choose me over and over and over…again
not perchance, but knowingly

the woman in me, woke up to long for the day
that you would choose me
that you would not let me down
that you could see the choice between…

and the choosing would be of me
so I could choose to lay down my armor
and hand you my heart brazenly

but you forced me to choose sunlight
absent you
and your not choosing me only forced me to see
the choice between…
choosing and struggling, having and wanting
you forced me to choose reality
redemption and serenity
you forced me to will a difference
to remove the armor for good

for me to choose me
for my love to heal me
to give my needs proper response-ability
and walk the good earth
free to choose
all the good and perfect already belonging to me

said you prefer that I come without my armor
I choose to not need any

Interlude

We are foolish to think our thoughts
are secrets covered by bones and limbs
and blood and skin
They manifest into living things
flowing in the ether
Determined,
they reach their destination,
seep into the skin and the breathing of our object
of affection
We call them to us…they come to us
it is no mystery
that from lonely, melancholy bodies
We can cast spells with our longing

After

After
the sounds of our cries
have ricocheted off the walls
and we've swallowed venomous words
sugar-coated with arsenic

After
I've borrowed your body
and you've burrowed in my body
all your false testimonies
and fragile promises
and broken songs

Only after
our fragments have settled,
our particles risen
our ashes blown away
and the smoke clears

There we will stand
beautiful
like Adam and Eve
before the blame
before the guilt
before the shame

humbled
naked
Who then, will bear our burden?

because there are rare moments
when I am soft enough to let you break me open
rare moments when you are soft enough to fill me full
scattered moments when
what we were is overshadowed by the light
of who we are in the moment
we should find a way to span our fragile moments
trusting brokenness

The Hours

All this fret over the 3 am hour–
apparently, that is when the desperation in longing
creeps in…wanting out…
but what of 8 am when the coffee brewed
by his hands
are missing
the aroma of nothing
is like a daunting disrobing of love
replaced by a shawl of loneliness
with a cup of emptiness

And what about 5 pm after a day of giving it all
and they give you more
but the one you need is not present
to soak up the heart's bleed,
I am my tourniquet
His vacancy a nervous undressing of affection

And yes, it is real when 10 pm finds you in your affliction
when we would take off our street clothes and settle
blessed in our bed…
engaged in a familiar nudity of raw unity
fondling thoughts, caressing verbs
but when I look to the right of me
the queen bed is hungry for our bodies

the pillow talk empty deprived
instead reciting apostrophes

The missing and the longing
prefers no time and favors no hour
no second is barred from italicizing his absence,
the void–it is all day for me
all day, not knowing what to do with my hands and my
mind–idle
all day, wanting something else to do with no one else to
pass the time
anything other than remembering recalling the living–dead
all day, wanting to forget the archives of a beloved history

If only we could dump the memories down the gar-
bage disposal
to turn forward the hands of time on every clock
to a moment when we can bear
aloneness

Untitled

I woke up this morning feeling unresolved
what does that really mean?
I woke up this morning afraid of my words
I'd much rather eat them than see them speaking into
my life
I woke up this morning uneasy
what does that really mean?
what is easy?
I woke up this morning and took a shower
in the shower I was wet, naked
and in the wet I was afraid of my nakedness
and my nakedness made me think
and as I thought I didn't like my thoughts
and I began to feel uneasy again
but what does that really mean?
My heart was not right
so make it right
I tried to pray and I prayed again
Your will be done on Earth as it is in Heaven
give me this day
who have I not forgiven?
what should I forgive?
I woke up this morning and I felt uneasy
over little problems and little people
I went to bed last night and it was not easy

why should it be?
and I woke up with it on me
This life it wants to make me hard
but this I cannot be
or could it be, this life is this life
what do I perceive?
who do I say I am?
And when I go to seek the world, who will I be?
I wore uneasy around my body
my suit fit uncomfortably, my blouse too tightly
I just want to breath
shake it off, shake it off–this feeling
I don't know what to do
do what you want to
decide,
so I slipped out of uneasy,
let it fall like a slip from the body
Went into the closet and wrapped myself
in a light cardigan the color of let me be
happy
please

Intermission

The beautiful things are everywhere
the lovely things…
delicate things,
fragile things,
vying for our presence
calling to our cognizance

They beckon us to notice
the pure of the ordinary
to sense
the prayer of the petal
thriving
admiring
Life

To lift our head,
and set our heart
to embrace every detail, every chance, every choice…

A beautiful life is not a dream deferred
it does exist
live in it

Love. Is.

A most delicate sacrifice.
A most fragile offering
of your own whole heart.

And you survive the pain of loving
through the joy of loving.
Let it break.
It is the only way.

Still in Orbit

all the nights we used to love
all the days we used to give
plagued me
I kept them tucked in shoeboxes, unopened emails
scattered love notes in papyrus cards
and the stars…
to the stars I cried
to the sun I prayed
wandering,
pretending to live
watching a world spin around me
life blurry
with everything
promising never again would he know me

until his signature slid down the inside of my thigh
never lasted three years, six months
and I don't know how many days
and he made up for every season he had been away
with each thrust and each kiss
I took to the moon for air
cajoling my wisdom as I turned on his axis
waking to morning nearby birds humming
from the window I steal a glimpse
outside the world still spins
inside the aroma of hazelnut coffee luring me
yes, still his love orbits me

Time Is a Wound

the kind of injury you suffer through from tiny lacerations
from the slicing of silk threads and soul ties
the kind of lesion that bleeds through your breast pocket
from a mangled heart and gashed hope

inside, a quiet explosion each time I laid eye on him
counting sands in the palm of my hand
rearranging piles of memories accumulated
paper cuts from torn letters and fallen love
splinters from broken pencils, words and vows
for every millisecond in every hour of every day
time didn't heal the wounds

passionately, I picked my scabs as a pastime
and inveigled him to taste my fresh blood
screamed in anguish in each interlude
swore into me a new chapter with him would not come
for I always knew time would never heal me
if I kept inviting him into my open wounds

I am a lover
not of things
but of heartbeats

don't ask me to fall in love
helpless
steady, I'd prefer to stand
intentional
so that in it, I may rise
perpetual

Buried a-Love

here lies loveless corpses
shrunken from fear
of flourishing
hear lies
dead promises
under fertile ground
howling to be let free
because in her heart she believes
when love...
we don't feed our demons
we free our angels
and because he allowed his beast to devour her
she buried hers alive
she had tamed it long enough
and wanted never again to draw to her another creature
and wanted nothing more than to attract a huMan
there would be no recompense of bleeding hurts
and possessed hearts
in the recesses she left them
in the garden of good and evil
she would be love and only love

But upon awake,
from a dead sleep
I realized,
I still walk naked in the catacombs of perished memories
waiting for any man to come rescue me…
with dead flowers
from a tomb of my late thoughts
I fell into my grave waiting for one to love me
And even beyond the interment
the need still holds me
refusing my spirit a rest in peace
But sleeping beauty rests no longer
I arise, hungry to be loved alive

Her Dedication

So for tonight, while I'm still sober,
I dedicate myself to me
To my words, my thoughts, my vicarious lives
my disasters, my rejoices, my void, my fullness
my infernal, blessed love to me
Because I can no longer dedicate myself to you

Never Another Again

But before I bury you
and perish the thoughts
there are words I have to say
Words like, it hurts to feel
hurts to believe
that the one you loved and love
would use you to dismiss you
Words like, it hurts to know
a human made of love could look you in the eye
and with meaningful words lie
because the lust in his heart is all he honors
and the fear in his chest palpitates louder
Before I bury you
and perish every thought of you
these words I give you
Words that say you will never use me again
for all the best I have been to you
for all the God I have been to you
for all the friend I have been to you
for all the encourager I have been to you
for all the mistress I have been to you
for all the loyal I have been to you
for all the woman I have been to you
for all the nurturer I have been to you
for all the grace I have been to you

for all the queen I have been to you
You will never use me again
the same breath we will never breathe again
the same love we will never embrace again
the same body we will never join again
the same bed we will never share again
the same moment we will never have again
There will never be another again
lemme say that again
You will never know me again
And I am well with this

Interlude

but you were never meant to be
a desolate place
for the nomads drifting
as fallen leaves
and lonely feathers;
you were always home and hearth
for the one love of your life

words Spirit whispered into me

Woman, Loosed

So what, he thinks you changed? So what?
When were his words ever gold to you?
And so what, he wants to degrade you?
It is because he cannot have you.
Yes, you were the best thing he ever had, but he never
knew you.
Then, you didn't know you. But now you do.
And he knows that you are well acquainted with the real
you.
The you with more grace left to want more and not accept
any less.
The real you who will not settle.
The absolute you who cannot be crushed by the words of a
man who is afraid of you.

Woman, you walk well in your shoes!
So what, he thinks you've changed; and not for the good
he adds.
And that's fine.
How dare you not disintegrate into ashes under every ven-
omous syllable from his tongue?
How dare you not fall apart without him?
Who are you to choose life without him over slow death
with him?
Who are you?

You are an intrepid lover!
The audacity of you to yet love again.
God has spoken over you. And you heard Him clear.
That man was not built to be with the worst you nor the best you.
That man is no match for you.
And the truth of who you are terrifies him.
You are the woman he loves…to hate.
You are the woman he can only dream to have again.
Because even at your worst, Woman, you were still his best

If the song could play forever
I bet you'd let it, you would
If our sheet music could sing forever
I bet you'd let it, you would
on and on
until we break down in the hum of the background
in the hum of our chaos
falling in the stanza of a long silence

we've been out of tune too long
never becoming one clef
I, alone on a stave,
harmonizing in an old alliteration...

...because I don't want to fight
anymore
I just want to love
More

Intermission

change keeps coming after me
finding me when I'm minding my business aimlessly
catching me in between the black and white
while I'm lounging in my shades of complacency
I gotta change coming and it's too big for my pockets
and it's gonna make a lot of sense to the ones who have
helped me
these brown eyes are wide open in my sleep
nocturnal dreams showing me I'm gonna change
become raw again, become new again
become all the things I am meant to be-I'm gonna be them
I'm changing the skin I'm in
changing the people I've been...tolerating
it's that simple–for me or forward me
I'm changing faces
trading ashes for beauty
and my lips will taste the change until I see it
I'm speaking a different life into my memory, my destiny
I'm changing places with me
leaving behind the small me, the wrong me, the hope-
ful me
coming into the big me, the right me, the promising me
I'm changing the things I used to do
to be the who I'm called to be
to have the things I want to have
and I'm not changing my mind until I'm a changed me

love
is what I offered
fear
is what he gave me
and all the heaven's rain
never washed away
our sins
nor our pain
though I, baptized
he would never circumcise
his heart to pure love me
like wilted flowers, jilted lovers
astray
with love is how I left him
with fear is how he wandered away

Thorn

Not a thorn on my side
but the thorn inside

That is what he became...
what I let him become
A sharp pain on the right side of my brain
to the left side of my body
A thorn on the inside triggered by sweet nothings,
any random vagary
On any given Saturday,
with aromatic smell
at the sound of any song when love was made
Pain would search me
grief come for me, from the deep of any memory
seized me like opportunity
And with it I'd play hide-and-seek
I'd hide behind it and seek outward for remedy
But nothing could please me or soothe me
I became a master at protecting the injury
A pain on the inside that would want to be the death of me
restrain me in emotional poverty
contain me in a heartless tragedy
So, I died
committed a suicide several times to come to new life
Naturally

emptied of any remnants of our duality
I plucked every root of that thorn
prayed it out of me, spit it out of me, washed it off every
limb and corner on my body that would think to hold on
to the fantasy I had so faithfully married
Breathing in reality
My thorn is no more

Complicated

With all this ugly
rooting up inside me
Will you still come
be beautiful with me?
Don't sift me for the desirables
ignoring my most valuable…
parts
And if you happen to taste the ugly
when you kiss me,
Don't spit out,
swallow me
Let me inside you

We are well deserving
of a human love that blends
our complicated into the simplest form
of soul to soul love
It won't be easy like Sunday morning
everyday
But it will be pleasing on most evenings
after dawning
after I've replenished my soul with a
good fixing of mourning…
the loss of all things bitter—
I can be sweet to you

You should just be complicated with me
on the odd days
I'll take the even

At the Altar
(Is Where You'll Find Him)

I left him at the altar
I didn't want to, but I had to
I left his memory, his affection, his curse over me
piled up at my feet

I wanted him too much
and the want consumed me
I loved him too much
and the love bruised me
He confused me
And I am not made to be confused
Confounded by this desire
It drove me to brinks of extinction
Why should I lose me?

I left him at the altar
sobbing quietly uncontrollably
Because it hurt every feeling in me
feelings he played like strings…second fiddle
when he said the object of love was me
I knew on the inside
he was the very thing I needed to release from
the spirit of me
I closed my eyes blurry

stinging from salt and mascara
I opened my palms sweaty
and I let him go

The choir singing
a congregation watching
some crying, others supplicating
But I walked away
withholding nothing

Love and Need, A Soliloquy

Love is, in fact an intensification of life, a completeness, a
fullness, a wholeness of life...
We do not become fully human until we give ourselves to each
other in love. *

That's what he said.
If only to live and breathe in this love,
I would, I have...
given morsels of myself away in ways that have left me
incomplete and missing.
My wholeness full of holes.
My intellect challenged through the encounters–empty.
My integrity diminished from the commune with
the counterfeit.
And yes, this mortal life, has been intense in the most
severe of ways,
to become human with one's who have not touched into
the deep of their own humanity;
those ones who do not weep, who disregard the
heart's bleed.
And when this one has run into shell upon shell of bodies,
climbing mere husk for skin, hiding shriveled beings, and
hardened hearts,
where does one such as self, search for love?

Because someone told me, I came into this world to
love indeed.
And with this my soul is well, but for the *but*...
But my soul cries out still, with who and for when?
The answer: from the within.
I look to the intensification and gratification
and actualization
of this full, robust, transformative love from none other
than my within.
To encounter, respond and commune with myself.
Until...unison.
Because despite the full bloom within,
I still seek to water the bud in another...
with-out me

He who said is Thomas Merton

Interlude

And then morning came
and baptized me
with an open heart
and renewed eyes

Future Perfect

I'm retraining my pen to record joy
to write of things not yet past
to create an art in living
to compose of imminent love transcendent
of flesh and time
I'm teaching my pen to recollect pieces of my whole
to paint bold pictures captured with
words of vivid colors
words of cherish, merriment, strength and resilience
words pregnant with hope and grace, love and legacy
I'm fine-tuning my pen
to be author of how I want this story to end
I'm daring my pen to predict an existence
far beyond my myopia
today's me boils with righteous envy
exercising aggressive patience
to reach the ultimate: she
who whips out her lovely pen
and designs at her every whim
a life worth living in the Master's garden

Paraphernalia

I own a piece of the sunlight
that falls through my window
and a corner of the moon
I sip on stars to get tipsy
when my dome gets too heavy

I own love in all the right places
in its rarest forms
even when it's mutated
please do not touch it
if you don't plan to give it back

I own living when I lay sight to seeing
hold heart to feeling
all the ups and downs and merry-go-rounds
I own strength to keep going
fertilizing the way
keep tilling

I own my color, my creed, my expressions
all my deeds
and whatever else I please
to include my music, my harmony
my memories, my sorrows
may I give you some please

I own it all briefly
these things and what more will come
like feathers and photographs
constant and random
precious possessions
blowing in the wind
of my everyday living

while still waiting
for someone's love
to come own me

Body

I live in my body
I've loved with this body
I've traveled miles and miles…
through his and his body
to return always to the inviolable parts of this body
honestly I'd be lost without my body
but by mercy still own my body
for so many times I gave of this body
trying to make us the perfect body
sullied this precious body
until finally grace broke apart this body
to refine the worth living in my body
cause when I was nobody
He gave up His body
not just another curvy, black body
but already a God body
so take your laws off my body
don't raise your hands to my body
and keep your limited words from my body
for while your eyes notice my earthen body
know I am the essence of a celestial body

Her Declaration

My body is not a cemetery of
dead things, dead men and dead relationships,

My heart is not a cemetery of caskets holding
fallen words, withered vows,
and decayed promises

I am a living love
overflowing with compassion
Harvesting love
Rejuvenating life

My body is a sacred space
My heart, a forgiving place
Welcoming
Open
I am so blessed and wonderful
Beloved in every way

Inviolable

how every unspilled tear has baptized the inside of
my spirit
dissolving every hard-bitter part that never had a lease
to lodge on the walls of my cellular being but took
occupancy
after every insult trauma heart contusion abuse misery…
all layered neatly under a mass of dressed up scar tissue
introducing herself as
dainty little me

the secrets I keep
resting peacefully alongside the marrows submitting to my
moral sinews civil warring
I ought remember to forget the casualties and celebrate the
victories and coronate the rebirth,
the nobility in me

because only I know
how He sat and watched me through the fire for the refin-
ing and purifying of me
until the very moment when I thought pain and suffering
would raze the sum of everything in me…
He saw His image reflecting and released me into the
world to share His glory in my story

only I know
what this life,
this earth,
this fragile chance means to me

Intermission

Somewhere in the dial of a clock,
in the rolling of a cloud,
stamped within dried concrete...
Someone made us to believe
waiting, waiting, waiting
for a better tomorrow
is the way to forsake a bitter today;
Well, I choose to stay in the sweetness of the hour
to savor everything in it
to sip it slow
come what may
With every breath drawn,
I owe myself that

Love Yourself to Life

Dear Us,

All this talk of love yourself, honor yourself, care
for yourself
but what does that look like?

It looks like you waking up every morning,
looking into your eyes in the mirror
and being grateful
that you can look into your brown eyes in the mirror
and see a face of innocence and wonder
life in the making
without judgement

It looks like gently, handling, cherishing and accepting
your body
because you yourself deserve your tenderness,
your heart deserves attention from you
your heart deserves kindness from you,
you deserve forgiveness from you
Above all, you deserve a second chance from you, or a
third...or fourth

It looks like you thanking God for your face, your smile,
your neck

your breasts are not too small, they're not too big, they are
perfect as they are

It looks like loving the sway of your waist,
the feel of your thighs, the arch of your feet
you really are made perfectly, relax into your body
It looks like loving the curves of your body,
loving the lines on your body,
accepting the wrinkles on your body,
forgiving the flaws on your body
Cause it's the one body you've got!

Touch yourself and hold yourself as you would your lover,
take your time, discover yourself, learn yourself,
affirm yourself
bring your broken, marred self back to the potter's house
and let him mold you again

It looks like looking back at where you were
and looking now at where you are
and thanking your angels for carrying you thus far
and further
Have confidence in, believe in, continuously;
your paths, the distance, the course
to your condition, your transitions and your destinations
All the ways you arrive belong to you and will work to
your becoming, your ultimate self

Loving yourself to life looks like gratefulness, carefulness,
and appreciation for everything;

Your love looks like feeding yourself with the foods that
nourish your body,
lend longevity to your heart,
and drinking the spring water to quench your soul
It looks like resting your head on a clean bed of soft sheets
keeping your atmosphere uncluttered and orderly to
encourage your inner peace

Indeed, your love looks like:
resting in the grace working around your life
Your love looks like letting love and light beam
through you
Your love looks like enduring resilience and every-
day surrender
Your love looks like you learning to trust in your divinity

And finally it sounds like you repeating these words to
yourself daily:
I know myself as love. I am love.
I know myself as loving. I am a lover.
I know myself in love. And I am my lover.

That is your call. That is your purpose.
To reach love, teach love and be love only.

Sincerely me…

Intermission

Don't let the Sun go down
unless you plan to stir up
your Love on the Moon
because we don't have Eyes to see
or Heart to know
what tomorrow will bring to us
For if we should have the chance
to arise in life's grasp again
it should be
to a gentle us

Looking into the full moon empties me of all my sorrows

To the One I Once Named Husband, An Apology Letter, Pt 1

A letter from a sincere part of me is overdue
It dawned on me, while light still shines
I should give every apology owed to you
while the unction fills me

From the beginning:
I am sorry for marrying you when I didn't know
how to choose a man to walk into my destiny,
for choosing you when I didn't know enough about me,
for choosing you...
when you should have found me

I settled for you because I was taught
to find a provider for my needs
but not a lover of my soul or a feeder of my spiritual needs
I made you my Husband
because they told me to hurry–I was getting too old
I am sorry, with a most sincere apology
for making expectations of you when I made not enough
of myself,
for forcing myself to love you and never letting it flow
from the deepest part of me

And I apologize because I didn't like you most days

cause you forgot to brush your teeth or
cause you didn't wash the dirt from under your fingernails
I'm sorry I didn't miss you when you left for work
though I became comfortable with you not being around,
I despised you for my loneliness, my brokenness
I blamed you for not being available to me,
for making a single wife out of me,
for not wanting to own responsibility for what, over time,
became the condition of our matrimony—
a secondary accessory to you
I made you wrong because you believed
what you were doing was right
I'm sorry for conditioning the love you gave me
decreasing it because it didn't look like the love I gave,
the love I believe I needed in return,
a love I once knew…
because truthfully I compared you to a love long
before you

And I apologize that I withheld my body from you
because I could not connect with you
With so much matter in between us,
I was disconnected from me…I couldn't join you

I'm sorry I felt I was just too good for you,
I was better than you deserved, even as I was not good to
me
I'm sorry for loving you when I felt like it,
too often in my feelings, finicky

I'm sorry I never loved you righteously,
I discounted your love, kept record of your wrongs,
deemed you unworthy because the truth is
I didn't believe I was worthy
I'm sorry I wanted you to validate me through prescribed
actions
and louder words, always wanting you to make it up to…
I wanted you to prove my worth to you–to me
I arrived with a deficiency, expecting you would invest
in me

I'm sorry I trained myself to love you through the years
but never learned how to speak the love language
you needed
that I worked at playing house but never mastered being a
wife, being your home

And I'm sorry I turned cold to you
because I let the temperature of another become my
barometer
sorry I could not be your soft shoulder
because I dishonored us and gave my body to another
I'm sorry,
I lost my identity and kept looking to you to recognize me,
I apologize because I let my void control me,
let my loneliness consume me
And because you could not fill me,
remove me completely away from you
And sincerely, I'm sorry
because I walked into marriage with you

like one who walks into a marketplace–
casually shopping unintentionally, hungrily…

That I never entered into covenant with you
before I entered into contract with you
That I wanted you to cover me when you didn't know
how to
That I wanted your prayer when I didn't have faith in you
I'm sorry, for conditionally–I loved you

And to this end:
I call you ex-husband
father to my one daughter, the youngest love of my life
I thank you for giving her to me
I accept responsibility for the demise of our matrimony
I drink up the cup of bitterness between us
and in exchange, serve you with a cup of sweet forgiveness

Please accept my apology
And as you become ready, forgive me

To the One I Once Named Lover—
Misnomer, An Apology Letter, Pt 2

A letter from a wiser part of me is overdue
At the dawn of my awakening it occurred to me,
to you
I should give every apology while grace still moves me

Sincerely, I'm sorry
for entertaining you when I had already
chosen a man to walk into my destiny
for attracting you,
because you smelled blood; I let you feast on me
for engaging you,
I took your interest in me as affirmation of my femininity,
my sensuality
for allowing you;
I mistook sin for flattery, disrespect for chivalry
I let me think you came to fill a void in me,
but desperation drove me and
distraction deceived me

And I apologize for making expectations of you
when I gave no honor to the ones made of me
for making false expectations of you,
I never earned any demand from you
for trying so hard with you
I opened up my heart to love you,

never letting it flow to the freest part of me–I needed my
love more than you
But I left it inside someone else long before you
didn't do the work to heal myself through

I'm sorry I wanted to be with you most days
and on other days could not bear the sight of you
could not bear the weight of you
It was my eyes I could not look into,
my insight I could not look into,
my heart I could not look into

I'm sorry I saw my guilt when I looked at you
I'm sorry I felt my guilt when I held you
that I wanted you to rescue me, I'm sorry that I
believed you
that I gave you access and permission to hurt me
I'm sorry I lost my identity
and expected you to give it back to me
that my heart was a messy place with shadows of men
who left gaping wounds long before you
that I wanted you to heal me too

And I apologize for treating you like a husband,
when it was clear, you would never make me a wife
I'm sorry I allowed you to enter into me,
creating a false sense of intimacy
simultaneously heightening a growing depravity
I gave you what didn't belong to me
My void, God-given, was never made to be filled with our
sin or your semen

I'm sorry I ran back and forth,
forth and back, never completely being still enough
to know—
I didn't know me
I'm sorry I expected you to see the worth in me
to fight the good fight for me,
to defend me, to honor, to love me
I'm sorry I was angry because you couldn't see
the sacrifice I made for you, for us to be
I never earned any demand from you—
I was never for you—that is the reality
And I took your degradation of me
I believed I deserved your humiliation of me
because I stepped out of my matrimony
How could I ask you to pray with me or discern
my sincerity

And I apologize
because I walked into adultery with you
like one who walks onto a stage play confidently...
out of her mind, out of her body...
believing the facade
That you never got to experience the real me
that I traded covenant love for condom love with you
that I traded my one extraordinary life for you
that I wasted too many acts with you
that I spilled too many words on you
that I cried too many tears for you
that I would have given more than I had left to be with
you

that I left myself with nothing because I poured it all
in you
I'm sorry I emptied myself when I should have been full
I'm sorry I brought to you brokenness
and expected you would make me whole
I'd been hollowed out years before you

And in the end:
I call you nothing
but an experience without enough words
one to mark and avoid
that we never procreated is a blessing
I thank you for everything and nothing
I recognize my error in expecting you to love me
To that end I bless you, I don't blame you
Love(her) was not your calling

I accept responsibility for your role in the demise of
my matrimony

Today, I look back at all the women I've been
and all the men you were
and know
we were always, as limited editions of ourselves,
never made to be whole with each other

I give you these apologies as I give them to me
and as you become ready, forgive me
and when you see the light, forgive yourself

A Kept Woman

He led me beside still waters;
still I strayed away
strayed to rough and rocky ways
thirsty again for Him

I want for green pastures
under my calloused, tired feet
I didn't know the journey would defeat me
didn't know the evil would come meet me
still, kept me through the path
through darkness in the valley
trembling, trusting
love and mercy always lurking unseen
steady comforted

from His table I want to eat
in His castle I want to sleep
where goodness and love
never tire to pursue me
knowing
with Him everything overflows in me

my God, my Guard and my Guide

Valor from the Valley

Joy didn't find me on the mountaintop
she met me in the valley
and peace didn't meet me on the mountaintop
he touched me in the valley
pain got me to the mountaintop
perseverance held me in the valley
triumph set me on the mountaintop
tears melded me in the valley
I, altogether on the mountaintop
was broken in the valley
with wisdom on the mountaintop
through understanding in the valley
I can shout it from the mountaintop
cause He showed me in the valley
Though you see me on the mountaintop
know–I was made in the valley

There was a time ago
when I made my worth
by the deeds of men
waiting for chivalry
wanting them to the see
the jades and emeralds
prove my value to me
disappointments and expectations
piled neatly...

Today, I know my worth
by the Love of God,
the grace I fall into daily
And as I breathe,
it is not a question of am I worthy
but more of an affirmation of Love me
just as I am in my totality

Dearly Beloved:
An Apology Letter to Me

Beloved, you have come a long way,
but you are not downtrodden
You have been through the fire,
and now your golden is pure

In this breath of time while the moment is now
allow me permission to apologize to the royalty in you
I am sorry for the men I have passed you through
I wish I would have heeded the voice of you
the one that echoed in the knowing of me…
admonishing me not to bring my pearls before swine
lest they trample me…and they did
walked away with my blood on their feet

Beloved, I'm sorry
I should have believed you, trusted you, befriended you
Instead, I best-friended false beliefs and vagaries
protected my fears and worshiped every part of me
holding empty
I slept with scorn for too many years
because that is what father gave me,
so that is the luggage I carried away with me
And I went out into the world unaware, unsure of
my being

attracting things to me...buried in my body

I'm sorry for not knowing
that each time I joined with a man
I picked up his baggage, a few of his demons
and traded traces of his past women disgraces
for a holier part of me
I'm sorry...

And I apologize
because I compared you to the girls in church
the ones I created perfect stories about
because they had husbands and not baby daddies
because they did it the "right" way
I'm sorry I attached shame to your story
I didn't realize how within it lived so much glory

And self, I'm sorry
I wanted you to be like the women of the world
the pretenders in the workplace
the ladies with the poker face
I coveted them, the way they planned matrimonial
festivities
cherry picked traditional families
showers and wedding cakes, I wanted all those things
I went against what God gave me
I struggled with our reality
making life a purgatory
Sincerely, I'm sorry that I made a habit of doubting
the divine in you

constantly vacillating from our false hope to our truth

Self, forgive me for thinking I was stronger...than life
for manipulating things to make them right in my sight
It was all make believe
an act to cover my sensitivity, my insecurity
Forgive me for not dealing with souvenirs the past
gifted me
before moving into seasons
that required so much of our presence
before relinquishing so many of the day to day presents
All the tomorrows I borrowed from
hoping to run away from yesterdays;
we lingered too long on unhealed wounds
and didn't get over so many offenses
I wish someone would have told me
to hold me through the growing pains
to stop looking to a he–
that I could regenerate and heal from within
Because all my running to a him always brought me walk-
ing back to me

Beloved, I apologize for rushing you
we should have taken our time, cultured our love
we should have did the time,
solitarily confined our heart until ready
because I could not stand my lonely
confused being alone for always waiting for a he to come
deliver me
never realizing my solitude was molding my attitude

that my aloneness, when I trusted, would bring me to
my wholeness

We should have rejected the doctrines,
objected the narratives,
contested the he said-she said should-ing on us
I'm sorry we believed everything they said
instead of questioning, finding, writing our own...words
our own interpretations, our own imaginations
We took theirs rather than creating our own templates

My mother's path is not my path, was not my way,
her dress was too small and her shoes too tight
I could not conform to the time of her life
I'm sorry I took her thinking and made it mine
I'm sorry I did the things my mouth vowed I would
never do
God had to show me myself
in the mirror–expose my weak righteousness
for a reflection of bona-fide strength
for a lifetime repentance

And beloved, forgive me
because when we stepped out
we stepped out on motherhood,
stepped out of our Godhood
selfishness made us abandon our maidenhood
But we know all things work together for our good

Beloved, I'm so proud of you

for becoming fireproof
for shining on despite all the dust,
the dirt you've crawled through
for finding your worth from the One true
Beloved, you are altogether beautiful;
My love, there is no flaw in you

I'm so glad through all the years
you collected your thoughts
you collected your tears
you collected your words
you collected yourself,
circumcised your heart
removed dead skin to emerge from your chrysalis
you've collected your life,
sifted through the lessons
to become a blessing

The excellent part remains: your story is not over
You have a wonderful life to live
and a powerful story to tell
Beloved, your best is yet to come
with all your love intact in you
This is your one perfect life!
Agree with it.

Beloved, I forgive you
And without restraint, I love you

Intermission

despite the reality
no one else on earth
moves to the metronome in your body
during the turbulence, the dark, the eruptions, the heat
directly in the face of life, disappointment, hope deferred
and even defeat
having done all you can to withstand
dance to the gospel rising on the inside of you

even if you are the only one hearing the beat

some will judge you
for harboring a bleeding heart

the ones with the crushed spirits;
dried up bones

they'll affront you with their lackluster love
and abhor you for loving too hard

because how could your frail body
contain so much passion

because where did you learn to forgive like this
and who taught you to honor your heart like this
to shed skin like this
renew soul like this…

those walking ashes will judge you
those cold ones, unopened and coagulated

they will want you to shut down
and clam up
focus on the loss
and memorialize the strain

they'll covet that for you
to become a visitant in your life

those fearful ones will want you to
bury and forget

but do not let them convince you
nor seduce you
to tame pain

all the elements you need to remember
to come out of your walls
to purge from your ever living

deliver them to their rightful owner

find yourself
passionate your existence

because the One who touches you
in the feelings of your infirmity
hath set you free

To return to Love

I will never ask for forgiveness for loving hard...
whatever that means

To Whom It May Concern,

I find it rather interesting
how so unconcerned we are with our conduct,
the ways we author ourselves in and out of souls and bodies

So unconcerned with the ways we treat/mistreat,
use/misuse,
profanely display disdain and disrespectful dereliction,
never once considering the legacy such actions
are carving and burning into the human psyche.

And I find it rather interesting how
we walk in and run out of living lives
with no CONCERN or aim
for leaving them more embolden than we found them…
(cause most of us would settle for, just leave me the same
as before if you can't leave me better than after you found
me)

Or that we have no concern for how a God in the sky
interprets our very own volition…
you know the will He gave us

No concern
for how heaven echoes
when we blaspheme with our bodies

and mutilate with our mouths
the precious beings He animated from dust
to become the affection in our lives

And even less concern for the angels encamped around us
cringing, crying for all the ways
we misappropriate
our spirit, our heart...

Then it was of no concern to you
how your true hue colored the world in me
No concern for the permanence of the impression
when you brandished I love you's, complacent pleas
and extravagant apologies
But as soon as the mere mortal puts her life into printed
calligraphy
suddenly–
you are concerned with the stage and the role you played
when you had your season with me

Just suddenly concerned with her skewed perception
drowning you in her prose and poetry

Perhaps if you considered your weight and your worth,
you would have acted differently then;
and perhaps if you were more concerned with your actual
character
than the mere portrayal,
you wouldn't go about daily life

dishing out your stains, serving up distrust, acting
less than...
when you are after all...a man

Perhaps if we considered that someone is keeping record,
someone is watching–we would treat each other better

But is that really the impetus we need?
That someone might one day join pen and paper to write
our shit for the masses to read...
How about just be a fucking good person?
That really works, you know!
And instead of showing your ass to loved ones, take it to
the damn toilet or the bath!

The moral of the story, and there are several:
1. If you don't want to see it in black and white: act right
*especially when dealing with a writer
2. What I think about you really doesn't matter, but what
you think of you does
3. It all belongs to God; you really should be concerned
with His judgement, not mine
4. Life goes on; move with it.

An Open Letter to Every Black Man Angry at His Choices

and taking it out on his woman,
taking it out on his children
I may have been your choice but I am not to fault
Man, stop blaming the woman,
it didn't work for Adam—it will not work for you

to every black man who's abandoned a black boy, a
black girl
know this: eventually, they will find you
better you come looking for them before they become you
or marry you
and the curse continues...
to every black man who is living
regretting
abandoning his seeds
return to their motherland and nurture the soil
there is yet time to reconcile
the time to forgive to *get* now

Man, what is the why behind your angry?
who did it to you that you should claim the right
to walk around this Earth punishing and unloving
all the feminine ones who come between you and your way
for what?

Man, what matter has come between us that vexes you to
the point of non-recognition?
a savage is not who you are called to be
shave the anger from your face so that I may see your true
identity
shed the pain from your skin
so that the world may perceive you clearly
so that I may know you
so that I may betroth myself to you
endow you with my charity
I am your lover, not your enemy
Man, respect me

You once laid down with me
you once craved me, cleaved your soul to me
and now you are perplexed by me, wrathful towards me,
vengeful to me
I did not do it to you
your greatest offence is from the loins of you
Black Man, please strip yourself of all the tired and weary
and pour love back in your bones
you are made of divinity
who told you, you were made for breaking down the good
thing God gave you
the women and children He blessed to you
to every black man, struggling within the sinews of
his body
there is yet strength in your tendons to bear the weight
upon you

there is yet patience in your tenderness to soften the world
around you
show yourself to God and I will show myself to you
stop hiding behind the feelings I too have from you
I am neither shaped nor built to carry your cardinal virtue

and Man, if after reasons and seasons come and gone
we do not flourish and succeed
as we had once anticipated and dreamed
do not turn from me as one who never knew or believed
that is the identity crisis you give to the child you leave
with me

instead, Man, keep in touch with your heart
because it is the scared, little boy in you
who will touch the little one outside of us
you don't need to be big and bad
just remember you are love and hope and faith
in the shape of a man
and we are looking towards you to shape our lives

to every black man
angry at his choice
you can choose again

Lesson Scorned

I've learned that you know no one until they turn on you
I've learned that you can sleep with your greatest enemy on
the smallest bed,
that you can blend bodies with your greatest foe and never
know until the day they come to reap all that you have
sown

I've learned that heart can be easily fooled when words are
many and said just right under moonlight
I've learned, there is nothing like a man scorned who keeps
score

And all these valuable lessons
I learned from the hands of men who touched me
from the mouths of men who said they loved me
from the bodies of the men who once claimed me

Oh, what love scorned does to the hardest of them
the toughest of them
changes them from frightened boys to spiteful men,
vengeful men
who come to pillage the hearts of women
cause they were never taught to
feel, forgive and forget from the love source in them

Yet still I learned through it all
bless them
because though they know what they do
forgiveness is for you, not for them
and vengeance is not yours,
God will better deal with them
He will heal them
therefore, release them

Your cup need not overflow with bitterness
sip from a sweet wine instead,
There is abundance of love to cover all
And through and beyond it all, you are priceless

Thou Shall Not F**k me and Forsake Me with the Same Body

Because we are grown enough to make wild love
and holy enough to commune
trusting enough to join our longing and desire in flesh
of love
But don't respect me and decide to neglect me
anytime soon after I've given you the gift of my intimate
body
My skin tone down to the marrow in every bone
rejoices to embrace you
Therefore, Man,
do not disgrace the sentiment in me by treating me like
some trick on Halloween
I know what I have and I know what I give
I should not live to regret the taking in of you,
so that I am forced to sieve the remnants of you from me

Please understand my act of opening to receive you
is no mere thing, or a one night thing
It is a sacrificial exchange
My womb is the most finite gift I have to bring
beyond the veil of my skin, a hallowed offering
to come into agreement with your entering my loving
My search for love begins in me and ends in you
that you would misuse my body

and forsake me
to obtrude your false consolations
only awakens a suffering within I can do without
Therefore, I say again, Man
Thou shall not entreat me to deplete me
I discreetly deny and boldly reject the desecration of my
body
or the judging of my emotions wrongfully
Though earthen vessel, my body is a temple
and I do know it
Therefore, treat me as holy ground

And she segued
from solitude to love
and from wanting to knowing
she writes her own love songs

Give away the four-leaf clover
pass by the shooting star
She is her first
and most perfect lover

The End

Wisdom...

A young girl growing up,
the world told me
until you become someone
who has done something,
you are not worth anything
And now today,
young girl grown wiser
I real-eyes my worth by who I Am
and by nothing that I've done
That I was born and choose to be
that I breathe the breath of life
that I bring value daily
declares I am worthy

Intermission

And suddenly without my knowledge,
without my begging,
while I was being,
Joy came upon me.

Good Morning

It's Not Popular

It's not popular, but I am my own happy ending
and it's not popular, but I am happy being me
and it's not popular, but I am a virtuous woman

It's not popular, but I am completely accepting of
my impurities
It's not popular, but I am the beloved child of God
and it's not popular, but I am a broken woman
and it's not popular, but I am a loving woman

It's not popular, but I am a sensitive woman
It's not popular, but I am the daughter of the Almighty
It's not popular, but I cry, I go crazy, I'm obscene
I say things,
I do things incongruent to my royalty

It's not popular, but I am peculiar,
no longer familiar with the lower things
no longer drawn to the former things

It's not popular, but I am well
and I am whole—alone
Nope, it's not popular, that I am blissed-out over me
Considering the good, the bad, the lovely
I'm not popular, I am me

Love Does

Only love can
wake me in the morning
with a burden to live curiously
Only love can
provoke me
incite me
continually
be compassion every day
make happy
Only love can surpass beyond our ugly
expose our beauty
Only love does
cover me
hold you
rescue me
defend you
Only love does
break our hard ground
overflow the hollow
make softer
grow our buds into blossoms
Love does render us so hopeful of things
to come
forgiving things gone
Love will

love you until you remember
to love yourself
then give it away
Only love does
endure
so that we may
bear it all

Though It Tarry...

This kind of love
the kind that opens you up
fertilizes the garden inside
spreading roots
seeds and flowers overflowing
words and thoughts emoting
closeness opening

This kind of love
the kind of love that transcends
rivers and lands
valleys and mountains
sidles around shoulders
slips in our mouths
seeps into pores
washes over the skin
reposes in the heart
glows the body

The only thing you wait for
a love seasoned
one love true
gives blood
sheds tears
pours living waters
refreshing the stream

The thing I wait for
for my love to face you
for your love to brace me
for love to eclipse us
walking in the dark
stars over head
hand in hand
as love becomes us

I can wait

Interlude

And I love that I could feel again
that I want to be alive in my life
again
I love that Finally Well became me,
no longer simple words eluding me—
but the way of living I deserve to be

I still have a joie de vivre—
they didn't take it from me;
It didn't go with them
I didn't give it away
still I carry it within
And it will always be my own to keep,
My own to live

I woke up this morning
to watch the sun rise from my brown eyes
I washed night from my face and body
ready and willing to take on abundant living
I took my time to savor the commencing
of the new day

Later, I relished a slow drive
and looking towards the sky
I imagined myself barefoot in the clouds
walking, being, reflecting
forgetting all the particular matter above the rain
under the royal cerulean blue glory
focusing on the auspicious view

Because walking on Earth can be so overwhelming at
times,
I tuck hope in the clouds

To remind me,
It is well with my soul
All is well with me
and over the horizon even when I can't see...
Courage, lovely heart
There is something greater propelling me
Love
and
new words not yet spoken
yet to be written
I look forward to living

Internally springing hope for my best

About Emmanuella Raphaelle

Writer, lover, inspirer, Emmanuella is a mother, daughter, sister and friend. She is an uncontrived, sensitive soul and a wonderful mess. But really, unpoetically, outside of words and imagery, she is a woman becoming. And when she is not writing words, she is writing a life worth living, full of laughter, loud love, vibrant colors and blooming flowers.

Some say she is an eccentric, phenomenal, bold and delightfully "NY rude" woman. Others say she is a gentle force to be reckoned with; one whose strength hides behind her humility. She knows because she asked, "What say you of me?"

But with a future yet to be written, she aspires to be known as a compassionate, prolific, author and world changer. She is the founder of Journal Journey, LLC, an indie publishing company for aspiring women authors. Emmanuella lives to leave a legacy of love, light and liberty every day. But while she's working towards that legacy, she enjoys a good bottle of wine, wearing cool shoes and colorful hair!

www.ingramcontent.com/pod-product-compliance
Lightning Source LLC
LaVergne TN
LVHW052340080426
835508LV00045B/2955